T0086961

Piano Sketches

Vitalij Neugasimov

Book 2

14 intermediate pieces for solo piano

MUSIC DEPARTMENT

OXFORD
UNIVERSITY PRESS

OXFORD
UNIVERSITY PRESS

Great Clarendon Street, Oxford OX2 6DP,
United Kingdom

Oxford University Press is a department of the University of Oxford.
It furthers the University's objective of excellence in research, scholarship,
and education by publishing worldwide. Oxford is a registered trade mark of
Oxford University Press in the UK and in certain other countries

This collection © Oxford University Press 2016

Vitalij Neugasimov has asserted his right under the Copyright, Designs
and Patents Act, 1988, to be identified as the Composer of these Works

Database right Oxford University Press (maker)

First published 2016

Impression: 5

All rights reserved. No part of this publication may be reproduced,
stored in a retrieval system, or transmitted, in any form or by any means,
without the prior permission in writing of Oxford University Press

Permission to perform this work in public (except in the course of divine worship) should normally be
obtained from the Performing Right Society Ltd (PRS) at www.prsformusic.com or
a local performing right licensing organization, unless the owner or the occupier
of the premises being used already holds a licence from such an organization.
Likewise, permission to make and exploit a recording must be obtained in advance from the
Mechanical-Copyright Protection Society Ltd (MCPS) at www.prsformusic.com or
a local mechanical copyright licensing organization

Enquiries concerning reproduction outside the scope of the above
should be directed to the Music Rights Department, Oxford University Press, at
music.permissions.uk@oup.com or at the address above

ISBN 978–0–19–341328–3

Music and text origination by Katie Johnston

Printed in Great Britain on acid-free paper by
Caligraving Ltd, Thetford, Norfolk.

Pieces from this collection originally published as part of
Pianoheads Collection 1 and *2* (2009 and 2010)

Contents

Country Fiddler	5
Annoying Fly	6
Funny Little Stride	8
Baby Star	10
Blue Rondino	12
Sweet Memories	14
Old Music Box	16
Space Wanderer	18
Menuet	20
Springtime	22
Your Eyes	24
Once Upon a Time	26
From Heart to Heart	28
Sonatina Polifonica	30

Composer's Note

Welcome to this short series of piano miniatures covering a broad spectrum of musical styles and gestures. Accessible yet engaging, the pieces should appeal melodically and harmonically to developing pianists, and provide opportunities for exploring musical textures and narrative while addressing technical points. They are written for player and listener alike, and hopefully inspire a sense of creativity and wonder at the palette of sound that is available to us.

This collection is dedicated to the memory of my beloved father, Vasilij Neugasimov. The pieces were inspired by my sister Liudmila Neugasimova, an outstanding piano teacher with over 20 years' experience; her encouragement and contribution were immense. I should like to thank, also, Martynas Vilkelis, who helped me to achieve my goal.

Country Fiddler

Vitalij Neugasimov

© Oxford University Press 2010 and 2016. Photocopying this copyright material is ILLEGAL.

Annoying Fly

Vitalij Neugasimov

© Oxford University Press 2010 and 2016. Photocopying this copyright material is ILLEGAL.

13
mf
16
Fine
p
19
cresc. poco a poco
22
D.C. al Fine
f

Funny Little Stride

Vitalij Neugasimov

© Oxford University Press 2009 and 2016. Photocopying this copyright material is ILLEGAL.

9
11
mf
p
13
f
15
mf
17
f

Baby Star

Vitalij Neugasimov

© Oxford University Press 2009 and 2016. Photocopying this copyright material is ILLEGAL.

21
rit.
a tempo
25
mp
29
33
p
36
rit.
pp
al niente

Blue Rondino

© Oxford University Press 2009 and 2016. Photocopying this copyright material is ILLEGAL.

14
mf leggiero
17
20
f
23
26
mp
p

Sweet Memories

Vitalij Neugasimov

© Oxford University Press 2010 and 2016. Photocopying this copyright material is ILLEGAL.

9
mp
mf
D.C. al Coda
11
CODA
13
p
16
rit. e dim.
pp

Old Music Box

Vitalij Neugasimov

© Oxford University Press 2010 and 2016. Photocopying this copyright material is ILLEGAL.

29
f
mp
Ped.
Ped.
Ped.
Ped.
34
39
p
45
mp
51
sf

Space Wanderer

Vitalij Neugasimov

© Oxford University Press 2010 and 2016. Photocopying this copyright material is ILLEGAL.

Poco meno mosso
17
p
Ped.
Tempo I
21
mp
25
29
mf
Ped.
32
rit. e dim.
mp
p

Menuet

Vitalij Neugasimov

© Oxford University Press 2010 and 2016. Photocopying this copyright material is ILLEGAL.

13
Fine
mf

Trio
17
p (pp)
senza Ped.

19
sempre staccato

22
senza rit.
D.C. al Fine

Springtime

Vitalij Neugasimov

© Oxford University Press 2010 and 2016. Photocopying this copyright material is ILLEGAL.

21
mp
mf
25
f
29
33
mf
36
39
mp
dim.
p

Your Eyes

Vitalij Neugasimov

© Oxford University Press 2010 and 2016. Photocopying this copyright material is ILLEGAL.

14
17
20
23
mp
27
rit.
pp

Once Upon a Time

Vitalij Neugasimov

© Oxford University Press 2010 and 2016. Photocopying this copyright material is ILLEGAL.

21
mp leggiero
25
29
mf
poco rit.
33
a tempo
mp
37
pp
rit.
Ped.

From Heart to Heart

© Oxford University Press 2010 and 2016. Photocopying this copyright material is ILLEGAL.

21
25
p
29
cresc.
poco rit.
mf
a tempo
34
p
rit.
38
Ped.

Sonatina Polifonica

Vitalij Neugasimov

© Oxford University Press 2016. Photocopying this copyright material is ILLEGAL.

22
mp
mf
26
tr
f
30
35
mf
40
f
p
44
cresc.
f